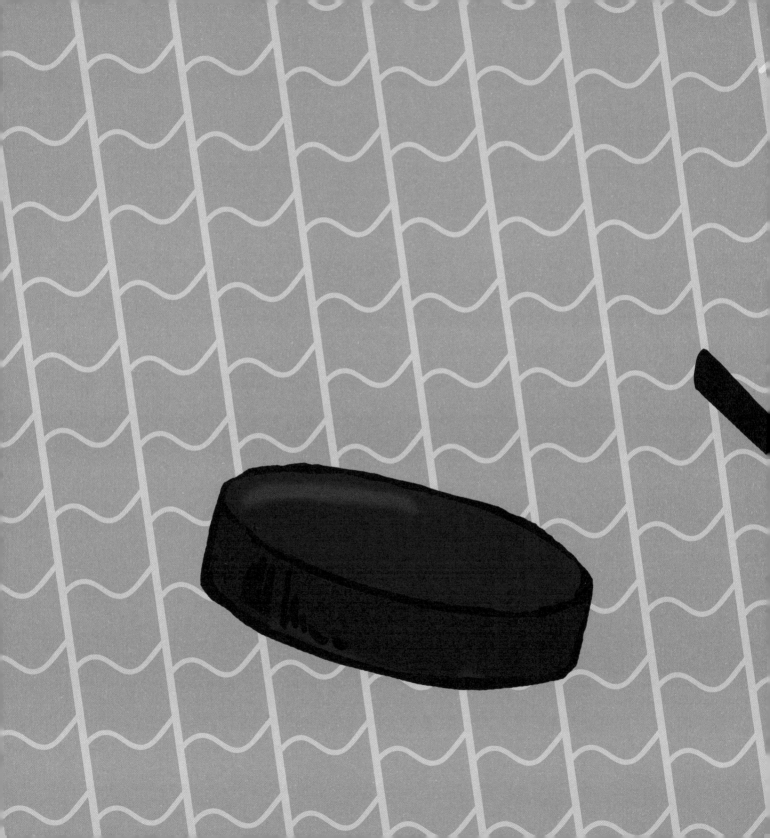

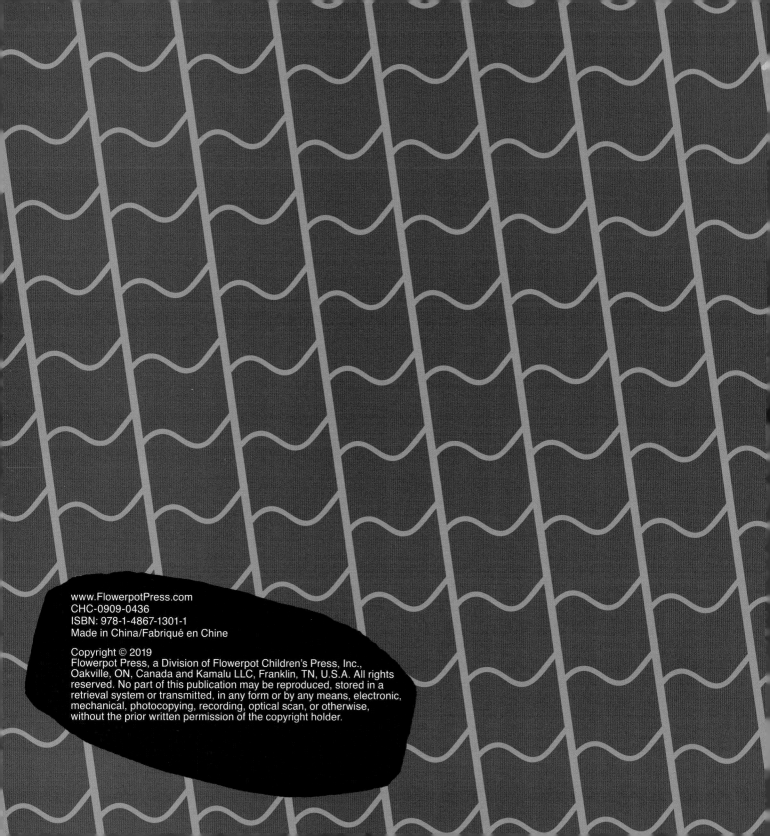

www.FlowerpotPress.com
CHC-0909-0436
ISBN: 978-1-4867-1301-1
Made in China/Fabriqué en Chine

Guess How Much I Love
HOCKEY

WRITTEN BY HARRY CAMINELLI ILLUSTRATED BY MARK KUMMER

much I **LOVE**

KEY.

Hi, I'm Ronnie.
I'm a rink rat. I help out
and hang out at hockey arenas!
I've hidden some really awesome facts
about hockey throughout this book
to help you learn more about
this cool sport!

PUCKS

Back in the day, pucks were made of wood or made from a rubber ball with the sides cut off.

Do you love hockey THIS much?

Pucks are frozen before games to minimize bouncing. Teams always keep a supply of frozen pucks so the officials can change them out during games.

A safety netting has been installed in many arenas to protect the fans from pucks going over the glass. Fewer injuries, good. Fewer free souvenirs, bad.

No, I love hockey more than that, because of the **PUCKS**. They are the six ounces of **FROZEN VULCANIZED RUBBER** you see flying around the rink and into the nets. Oh yeah, **NETS**! **SIX FEET WIDE** and **FOUR FEET TALL**, the net stands with **MESH**, is surrounded by a **CREASE**, and is guarded by a **GOALIE**.

No, I love hockey more than that, because the **STICKS** are awesome! There are **LEFTIES**, **RIGHTIES**, and **STRAIGHTIES**. Did you know they used to be made from **IRONWOOD** because it was so strong? Then they used lighter woods, such as **ASPEN**, then **FIBERGLASS**, and then **ALUMINUM** with **REPLACEABLE BLADES**. Most players today use **COMPOSITE STICKS**, because they are light and can add speed to their shot.

Sticks have flex ratings that go from super flexible to crazy stiff. The style and size of the player will determine which stick is right for them.

Players tape the blade of their stick to prolong its life and to create friction between the stick and the puck.

Do you love hockey THIS much?

No, I love hockey more than that, because you get to wear the coolest **EQUIPMENT**! It's like a **SUIT OF ARMOR** to protect you from the puck, sticks, boards, ice, and other players! **SKATES** are cool, but there are also **SHIN PADS**, **SOCKS**, **PANTS**, **JOCKS**, **JILLS**, **HOCKEY GITCH**, **SHOULDER PADS**, **ELBOW PADS**, **NECK GUARDS**, **MOUTH GUARDS**, and **HELMETS**. I almost forgot the **GLOVES**! They make you **FEEL** and **SMELL** like a real hockey player.

Helmets are often called "salad bowls" or "buckets."

The "celly" is the celebration done after a player scores.

No, I love hockey more than that, because of all the **DIFFERENT SHOTS**: **WRIST SHOTS**, **SNAP SHOTS**, **BACKHANDS**, **ONE-TIMERS**, and yes, **CLAPPERS**, also known as **SLAP SHOTS**! For **WRIST SHOTS** you pull the puck quickly along the ice and roll your wrists when you let it go. **BACKHANDERS** are when the puck is on the opposite side of the curve, and they are great for clearing the zone in a hurry or shooting high when close to the net! **ONE-TIMERS** are one of the **TOUGHEST SHOTS** to make and are even tougher to save. A player with the puck passes it to an open **TEAMMATE** who times the shot with the arrival of the puck. Here it comes—and **WHAMMO**!

No, I love hockey more than that, because of the **GOALS**. The goals are my **FAVORITE**! **FIVE-HOLE** means going between the goalie's legs, **TOP SHELF** means into the upper part of the net, and the best ever—**BAR-DOWN**. That's a shot off the crossbar and into the net. There are also **SHORTHANDED** and **POWER PLAY** goals, depending on whose team has a player in **THE BOX**. **BREAKAWAY** goals are one-on-ones and "**LIGHTING THE LAMP**" refers to the goal light coming on.

Wayne Gretzky holds the record for the most goals scored in the NHL with 894.

No, I love hockey more than that, because you can play all kinds of **POSITIONS**. You can take **FACE-OFFS** and **SKATE EVERYWHERE** when you play **CENTER**, or you can help out up and down the sides as a **LEFT WINGER** or **RIGHT WINGER**. You can be a **GRINDER** in the corners or a **SPEEDSTER** up the middle. You can also play **DEFENSE** and get the puck away from your net and out of your end. Best of all, **ANYONE CAN SCORE**—even the **GOALIE**!

Do you love hockey **THIS** much?

No, I love hockey more than that, because I love the **PLAYS** our coaches show us. They teach us about **FORECHECKING**, **BACKCHECKING**, and setting up the box so the other team can't get to our net. We **CYCLE THE PUCK** by quickly passing it and moving around in the other team's end. Going around your opponent by moving the puck from side to side is called a **DEKE**. There are also **TOE-DRAGS**, when a player fakes one way with their forehand and with the tip of the stick brings the puck across the opposing player to skate by them. **SEE YA!** And I almost forgot about **REBOUNDS!** They happen when the goalie makes a save but can't cover the puck, giving up another chance for a shot.

PK is short for penalty kill. It happens when a team has a player in the box serving a penalty.

To avoid being "deked-out," defending players watch the opposing player's chest, not the puck. "Deke" is actually short for the word "decoy."

Power plays happen when one team has more players on the ice due to one or more players sitting in the penalty box.

No, I love hockey more than that, because I **GET TO PLAY WITH MY FRIENDS** and **MAKE NEW ONES**! As a hockey player I learn about **SPORTSMANSHIP**, trying my best, and how to be a **GOOD TEAMMATE**. Both **BOYS AND GIRLS CAN PLAY** at different levels depending on their skills. You can play hockey for **FUN**, at **SCHOOL**, and even as a **PROFESSIONAL**.

Practice is where players develop their skills. Games are where they show what they've learned.

In 1942 the NHL consisted of the "Original Six" teams. In the 2017-2018 season the Vegas Golden Knights were added, bringing the league total to 31 teams.

No, I love hockey more than that, because OLD ARENAS smell great! The GIANT SCORE CLOCKS are the coolest, and there are always CHAMPIONSHIP BANNERS hanging from the rafters. There's also a WALL OF FAME full of local hockey heroes and TROPHIES. I really love the BRIGHT LIGHTS and 200 feet of OPEN ICE. There's a RED LINE, BLUE LINES, and GOAL LINES. The teams sit on the players' BENCHES, but if you get a penalty it's off to THE BOX. Some players call it the "SIN BIN."

Do you love hockey **THIS** much?

One of the biggest upsets in Olympic hockey history was between the Soviet Union and the United States, and it is commonly known as the "Miracle On Ice." It was named for the moment when announcer Al Michaels shouted with three seconds left, "Do you believe in miracles?!"

No, I love hockey more than that, because the ANNOUNCERS SAY OUR NAMES so everyone in the arena can hear! They INTRODUCE the PLAYERS, tell the FANS about GOALS, ASSISTS, and even the PENALTIES. Sometimes they REMIND EVERYONE when there is only a minute to play in the period. And the MUSIC is awesome! ROCK SONGS, DANCE SONGS, RAP SONGS, COUNTRY SONGS, and HOCKEY SONGS. There is also the NATIONAL ANTHEM. Standing at attention while your country's anthem is playing is amazing and listening to your OPPONENT'S ANTHEM is pretty cool, too!

Organ music is still played in some arenas, but many have opted for song lists requested by the players or hometown crowd.

"He shoots, he scores!" is a term created by Canadian broadcaster and play-by-play commentator Foster Hewitt.

The Stanley Cup was first won in 1893.

The Hart Memorial Trophy is presented to one player deemed most valuable to their NHL team.

Do you love Hockey **THIS** much?

No, I love hockey more than that, because you can win amazing **TROPHIES**! First in the **DIVISION**, **TOURNAMENT** winners, and **LEAGUE** champs usually get some pretty cool hardware. Players can also receive **MEDALS** for **SPORTSMANSHIP**, contributing to the **TEAM SUCCESS**, overall **IMPROVEMENT**, and sometimes just for showing up. **THE STANLEY CUP** is one of the oldest trophies in professional sports and the hardest one to win.

An octopus was thrown on the ice to represent the eight wins needed for a team to win the Stanley Cup in two, best of seven series. Nowadays, an NHL team needs to win sixteen playoff games to hoist the cup.

YES!
I love hockey that much, because it is awesome and **THE COOLEST AND FASTEST GAME ON EARTH**

HOCKEY LINGO

ASSIST the one or two passes leading up to a goal.

BACKCHECKING when the defending team skates back to protect their net and regain possession of the puck.

BASKET another name for the net.

BARN an old arena.

BISCUIT another name for the puck.

BLADE the part of the stick used to handle, pass, and shoot the puck.

BLUE LINES lines on the ice indicating the boundary of a team's zone.

BOARDS the white walls that surround the ice.

BUCKET another name for a helmet.

CENTER ICE the circle in the middle of the rink used for face-offs at the beginning of every period and after a goal is scored.

CLAPPER another name for a slap shot.

CREASE the area in front of the net.

DANGLE when a player skates around another player on the opposite team, making their opponent look a bit silly.

FACE-OFF when the referee drops the puck between two players to start the next play.

FLEX-RATING the number on a stick based on how flexible it is.

FLOW a hockey player's long hair.

FORECHECKING when offensive players attack the defending team to create a turnover.

GOAL LINES the red line that spans each end of the ice and the net.

GRINDER a player that likes to hit, bang, and crash opponents to cause turnovers and take possession of the puck.

GITCH the underwear worn beneath a player's equipment

LEFT WINGER the forward player that covers and controls the left and center lanes of the ice.

LEFTIES refers to a left-handed stick or players that shoot left.

LINE CHANGE happens when players from the ice go to the bench to be replaced with teammates who have fresh legs.

NEUTRAL ZONE the 50-foot area on the ice located between both of the blue lines.

ONE-ON-ONE when a player with the puck breaks away from the pack and has no one between them and the goalie.

OVERTIME (OT) the time after regulation play that continues until a goal is scored.

PENALTY BOX (THE BOX) the small area where players sit to serve a penalty.

PENALTIES a rule infraction. It can be a minor penalty, a major penalty, or a match penalty.

RED LINE appears at center ice and divides the ice into two halves.

RIGHT WINGER the forward player that covers and controls the right and center lanes of the ice.

RIGHTIES refers to a right-handed stick or players that shoot right.

RINK RAT the term given to a kid that hangs out at the rink a lot.

SHORTHANDED when a team has at least one player in the penalty box.

SHORTY a goal scored by a team that is shorthanded.

SLAP SHOT a difficult shot in which the player brings the stick off the ice in a big wind-up, then quickly brings it back to hit the ice behind the puck to create a "whip" action in the stick.

SNIPE a well-placed shot that ends up in the net.

SPEEDSTER a fast skater.

TOP CHEESE/CHEDDAR a shot that goes into the top part of the net.

TWIG another name for a hockey stick, though few are actually made of wood.

W short for win.